RODGERS & HAMMERSTEIN HITS

arranged for brass quintet
by Charles Sayre

easy level

THE CANADIAN BRASS

CANADIAN
BRASS
SERIES OF
COLLECTED QUINTETS

HAL•LEONARD®
CORPORATION

7777 W. BLUEMOUND RD. P.O. BOX 13819 MILWAUKEE, WI 53213

C A N A D I A N B R A S S
SERIES OF
COLLECTED QUINTETS

RODGERS & HAMMERSTEIN HITS

arranged for brass quintet
by Charles Sayre

contents

3   **Blow High, Blow Low**
     from *Carousel*

4   **Edelweiss**
     from *The Sound of Music*

5   **Honey Bun**
     from *South Pacific*

6   **Oh, What a Beautiful Mornin'**
     from *Oklahoma!*

7   **Oklahoma**
     from *Oklahoma!*

8   **You'll Never Walk Alone**
     from *Carousel*

Welcome to the new *Canadian Brass Series of Collected Quintets.* In our work with students we have for some time been aware of the need for more brass quintet music at easy and intermediate levels of difficulty. We are continually observing a kind of "Renaissance" in brass music, not only in audience responses to our quintet, but to all brass music in general. The brass quintet, as a chamber ensemble, seems to have become as standard a chamber combination as a string quartet. That could not have been said twenty-five years ago. Brass quintets are popping up everywhere — professional quintets, junior and senior high school ensembles, college and university groups, and amateur quintets of adult players.

We have carefully chosen the literature for these collected quintets, and closely supervised the arrangements. Our aim was to retain a Canadian Brass flavor to each arrangement, and create attractive repertory designed so that any brass quintet can play it with satisfying results. We've often remarked to one another that we certainly wish that we'd had quintet arrangements like these when we were students!

Happy playing to you and your quintet.

— THE CANADIAN BRASS

BLOW HIGH, BLOW LOW
(From "CAROUSEL")

3

1st TRUMPET

Lyrics by Oscar Hammerstein II
Music by Richard Rodgers

Intro
Lively March Tempo (♩ = 120)

EDELWEISS
(From "THE SOUND OF MUSIC")

1st TRUMPET

Lyrics by Oscar Hammerstein II
Music by Richard Rodgers

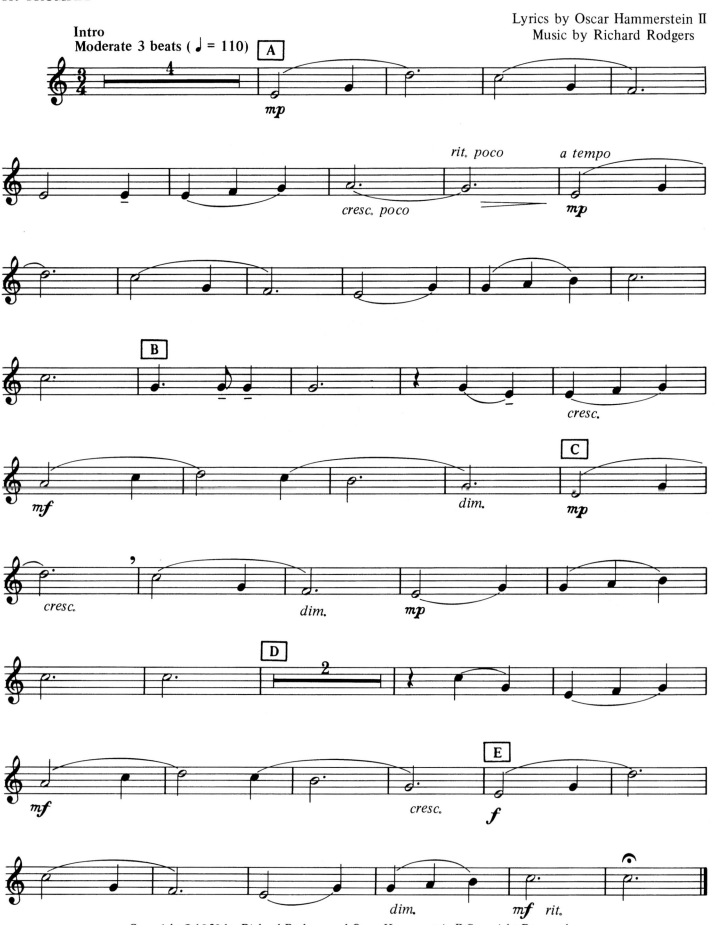

HONEY BUN
From ("South Pacific")

5

1st TRUMPET

Lyrics by Oscar Hammerstein II
Music by Richard Rodgers

OH, WHAT A BEAUTIFUL MORNIN'
(From "OKLAHOMA!")

1st TRUMPET

Lyrics by Oscar Hammerstein II
Music by Richard Rodgers

OKLAHOMA
(From "OKLAHOMA!")

1st TRUMPET

Lyrics by Oscar Hammerstein II
Music by Richard Rodgers

YOU'LL NEVER WALK ALONE
(From "CAROUSEL")

1st TRUMPET

Lyrics by Oscar Hammerstein II
Music by Richard Rodgers

*Legato phrasing throughout

U.S. $7.99

50488766

ISBN 978-1-4584-0160-1